Online Dating: Successful Methods that Work

How to Find Your Soul Mate Online

Jane Wymer

This book is dedicated to everyone searching for their soul mate. May love and happiness find you.

Copyright Act of 1976, the scanning, uploading and electronic sharing of any part of this book without the explicit written consent or permission of the publisher constitutes unlawful piracy and the theft of intellectual property.

If you would like to use material or content from this book (other than for review purposes), prior written permission must be obtained from the publisher.

You can contact the publishing company at admin@speedypublishing.com. Thank you for not infringing on the author's rights.

Speedy Publishing LLC
40 E. Main St., #1156
Newark, DE 19711
www.speedypublishing.co

Ordering Information:
Quantity sales; Special discounts are available on quantity purchases by corporations, associations, and others. For details, contact the "Special Sales Department" at the address above.

This is a reprint book.

Manufactured in the United States of America

Table of Contents

Publisher's Notes i

Chapter 1: Introduction to Online Dating 1

Chapter 2: Online Dating – How to Be Successful at It 3

Chapter 3: The Pros and Cons of Online Dating 6

Chapter 4: Choosing the Right Online Dating Site for You 9

Chapter 5: Getting Started 13

Chapter 6: Choosing Your Profile Picture 19

Chapter 7: What Are People Looking For? 22

Chapter 8: Take Action and Initiate Contact 25

Chapter 9: Sending Effective Emails 29

Chapter 10: A Little Bit of Charm Can Go a Long Way 32

Chapter 11: Don't Let Fear Paralyze You 35

Chapter 12: Meeting for a First Date 38

Chapter 13: Online Dating Tips to Remember 41

Chapter 14: Are Online Dating Tests Helpful? 43

Chapter 15: Final Thoughts on Online Dating 45

Meet the Author 47

More Books by Jane Wymer 49

Publisher's Notes

Disclaimer

This publication is intended to provide helpful and informative material. It is not intended to diagnose, treat, cure, or prevent any health problem or condition, nor is intended to replace the advice of a physician. No action should be taken solely on the contents of this book. Always consult your physician or qualified health-care professional on any matters regarding your health and before adopting any suggestions in this book or drawing inferences from it.

The author and publisher specifically disclaim all responsibility for any liability, loss or risk, personal or otherwise, which is incurred as a consequence, directly or indirectly, from the use or application of any contents of this book.

Any and all product names referenced within this book are the trademarks of their respective owners. None of these owners have sponsored, authorized, endorsed, or approved this book.

Always read all information provided by the manufacturers' product labels before using their products. The author and publisher are not responsible for claims made by manufacturers.

Chapter 1: Introduction to Online Dating

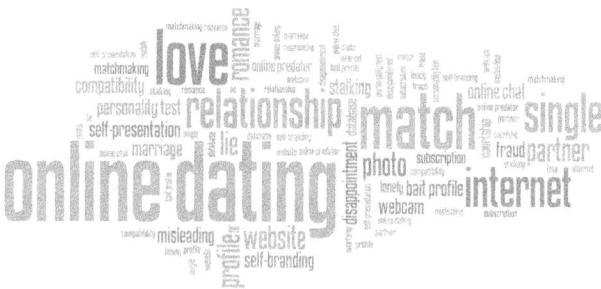

So you are thinking about online dating? Will this be a successful endeavor for you? Or, will you simply pick any online dating site that shows up and register? Will you wait for that right person to come out and find you?

When it comes to online dating, it is up to you to make it happen. There is no reason why anyone that is looking to find their soul mate or anyone just looking to meet a great guy or gal should not be able to do just that. The problem is that many of us leave it to the other person to make the move and make it all happen.

What you will learn in this book is simple. You are going to learn how to be successful at online dating with insider tips and tricks to make yourself and your chances of success better.

Is there something that you can do right now? Take the time to read everything in this book. It will allow you to make the right decisions about your online dating experience.

What you will learn is that at each step in the process there is something else for you to do and accomplish. When you put the pieces of the puzzle together, you will find yourself winning at successful at online dating.

How do you find success? Dating success is all about finding the happiness you are after while being safe during the process. If you want to be one of those people that say that they met their soul mate on the web, then take the tips and tricks in this book to heart and follow them.

Chapter 2: Online Dating – How to Be Successful at It

Online dating is something that anyone can do, but not everyone is successful at it. Let's think of this as building a business. If you want to be successful at your business, you have to work it from the beginning, nourish it throughout its hard moments and then know how to make your mark.

In online dating, to be successful, you need to start off right, build your profile honestly but correctly and then find and secure the rewards that are out there. You need to understand that valid tips and tricks will help you be successful at online dating.

Throughout this book you will have tips and tricks offered to you. Yet, before we can tell you how to take your online dating experience to success, we need to map out where we are going.

Your Goals

The first thing you need to do is make goals. What should you include in these goals? Ask yourself the following questions.

- What am I looking to achieve during my online dating experience?
- What is the method (dating site/s) I will use?
- Who or what am I looking for specifically?
- What am I willing to do to make it happen?
- Can I dedicate time to making it happen?

When you ask yourself these questions, jot down your answers. You will want to come back and refer to them later. Why should you answer the questions above? Developing goals for online dating is essential. In fact, it is your first tip. Without detailed goals, you will not do all that it takes to be successful.

If you do not have goals, you probably will not spend enough time on your profile. If you do not have goals, you probably will not take the time to seek out others. And, if you do not have the right goals in place, you won't take that all important first step of calling on someone that you are interested in.

After you have determined what your goals are, next determine what you will do to meet them. Here are the first things you need to commit to in order to be successful with online dating.

1. Spend a good amount of time developing a profile.
2. Spend at least a few hours a week looking for people that you would like to meet.
3. Spend a few hours a week sending off emails to those that you are interested in.

When you do these things, you are going to be steadily working your way to finding that perfect person to fill all the important parts of your life.

The upcoming chapters will touch on different things that will enhance your dating experience. The focus of this book is not to change you, but to showcase yourself to attract people that will like you for who you are now.

Being You

Before we get started, let's take the time to make sure you know the importance of being you. If you are someone that thinks they have to change who they are to be successful at dating, you will always fail.

Instead, you need to be you. You will learn how to enhance the way you portray yourself to others so those that would be interested in a person that has your qualities and characteristics will be lured to you. We are not changing you. Don't try to create a profile or even a persona that is not genuine to whom you are. It just will not be successful.

Follow the tips in this book to achieve online dating success.

Chapter 3: The Pros and Cons of Online Dating

You have a good idea of what the pros and the cons of online dating are right?

Pros:

- You get to meet others from around the world when it is convenient for you.

- You get to find that right person for you without having to deal with the bar scene or with blind dates.

- The pressure is lower as emails are easier than phone calls.

- You can find people online that are just like you, that already possess the qualities that you are after. No more dealing with situations where you meet people that are nowhere near someone you are interested in.

- You get to handle online dating the way that you want to.

- It's safer.

- There are more possibilities.

- Those are just a few of the benefits that are out there when it comes to online dating. Yet, there are some things that are not necessarily good things.

Cons:

- You are not seeing these individuals in person for the first time.

- You may not be able to meet them locally for a while if they do not live near you.

- You have to count on what they tell you or provide about them in their profile is actually true.

- It's scary to take that first step.

- You have to pay for a membership to meet others.

Those are just a few of the different cons that you may be facing. Take into consideration that you may have specific cons that are not listed here. Nevertheless, the next tip is what will help you to get the most out of online dating.

Analyzing the Good and the Bad

Each time that there is a negative comment in your mind about online dating, figure out the benefits it can offer.

For example, one of the problems that many have is paying for a membership. While no one likes doing that, think about it this way. If you pay for a membership, you don't have to pay for drinks or dinners with others that you didn't connect with. It is more affordable, actually, to meet with people that you have already determined are right for you.

Another thing people say about online dating is that they just don't want to take that first step and contact the other person. No problem. A chapter is dedicated to learning how to converse with others for the first time. And, you will learn how to make this something that is beneficial to you.

There are many benefits to online dating. There are plenty of opportunities for you to find the right person out there. Yet, you can sit there and worry about it, or just get out there and do it.

If you want to find success in online dating, you need to commit to doing it. You are about to learn how to do that, but remember that it is a package deal. You must take action to make online dating work for.

So, where does that leave you?

Your first step is to commit to online dating. It is fine to give yourself a time frame, but be sure it is long enough to give the process a chance. If you try online dating you need to make a commitment and truly dedicate time to the process. When you are committed, you are more likely to have a positive experience from the process.

CHAPTER 4: CHOOSING THE RIGHT ONLINE DATING SITE FOR YOU

There are many online dating websites and each of them offers something unique and different than the next. If you find yourself dealing with the wrong site, you may find yourself wasting your time.

First, think about who you are and who you would like to meet. This will help you determine what the best online dating website is for you.

Who Are You?

Some online dating sites are set up based on things such as function as well as popularity. Many of the big online dating sites do offer benefits of being able to allow you to meet a wide range of people. If you are looking for someone special, though, you may find yourself facing a bit more trouble with these sites.

Instead of selecting just any online dating site, if you do have special characteristics that you are interested in, make sure you venture to websites that cater to just that.

For example, there are some very popular websites set up for online dating that offer their pitch to those of a specific race or religion. If you are interested in only finding Jewish people to date or you really only want to find an Asian person, these sites can help you to bring you closer to your goal.

If you do have a specific preference, using these sites is fine. Yet, keep something in mind.

The number of people that visit an online dating website is also an important thing. If the site only has a handful of people on it, your chances of finding someone that fits with you perfectly is going to be more of a challenge.

In other words, your goal should be to find a website that is both popular enough as well as specific enough for any specific characteristics that you are interested in.

What the Site Does for You

Now that you know what kind of online dating website you are interested in, it is time to begin looking for the most ideal choice. Although this can be difficult at first because there are so many out there, you will want to look for some key features in any online dating website that you decide to work with.

If you choose to work with an online dating website that does not offer these key ingredients for success, you are less likely to find yourself benefiting from it or you may just have a more difficult time at it.

So, what is it that the website should provide to you? Here are some key aspects to take into consideration.

1. It should provide a good range of different types of people (unless, as described, you are looking for specific characteristics only.)
2. It should have an easy to use interface that is not too complex for your understanding. To judge this, make sure you take a look at what the website offers in their introduction. Is it hard to find information or to navigate the site?
3. It should allow you to set up a pretty complex profile, something that will be discussed more in the next chapters.
4. The website should be affordable. You do not want to destroy your finances because of online dating.
5. You should be able to tour the website and get to know how the system works before you commit to it. If you do not know what's out there, you cannot make good decisions about if it is right for you.

The tips that you learn to implement from this book will require you find quality website dating adventure.

After you have selected your online dating site, you can begin putting it all together. Although it may seem like it is something simple, it should be taken quite seriously. If in fact you just brush through it, what impression will your online dating profile give to others?

The features, information and the guidance that you get from online dating websites is all put in place to provide you with the most ideal environment to grow your profile. We say grow because it will in fact be something that you need to dedicate your time and energy too and therefore grow into something that is worthwhile to you.

Take some time to browse several websites out there. Make sure that you understand the lingo and the membership packages. Yes, it does make sense to spend some time comparing features and costs as it is going to be essential for you to do this if you plan to find the best opportunity for you.

Cost is important, but do not be fooled into believing that the lowest costing online dating site will provide you just as good of service. On the flip side, do not think that the most expensive online dating service will provide you with the best service either. In most cases, the middle of the road is the place to be.

Get the Most for Your Money

Finally, we do want to make a note of something here that you need to take into consideration. If you will be using an online dating website to help you to find someone to meet, it makes sense that you get the most for your money. How do you do this?

First off, you insure that you are allowing yourself enough time to work on your online dating relationship. You will need to commit some time to online dating if you wish it to be a successful adventure and one that really does pay off the way you want it to.

But, more so than that, you also need to use all of the tools and features that they are giving you. In reality, the online dating site does have quite a bit at stake in you working with them. If you find success, you are almost guaranteed to provide them with more clients through word of mouth business.

Therefore, each sites features and tools are meant to help you to get the most out of your experience. If the membership plan you have selected does not include all of the bells and whistles, don't sign up for them just yet. Instead, read through the material in this book first before making that decision.

Chapter 5: Getting Started

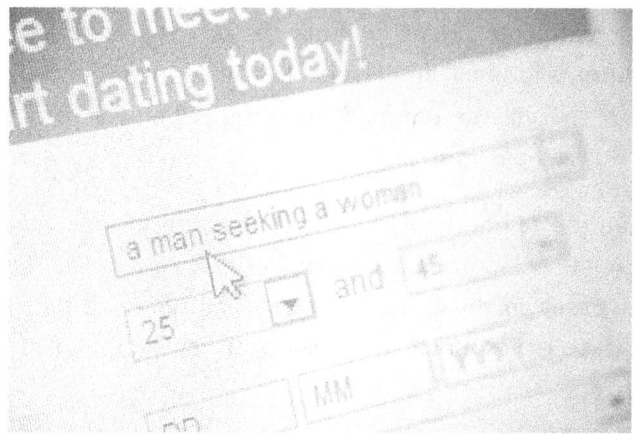

In this chapter, we will talk about one of the foundations of any online dating experience. Without this being put together well, you will not attract the right people and therefore are not likely to get the results you are after.

Your profile is the key to finding the right guy or the right girl. In short, there is no chance that you will find someone out there on those lists of thousands of people without having a great profile.

What's A Profile?

Most of the online dating communities use a profile as the way to meet others online. After you register with your online dating site, your first step will be to complete your profile. Is there one aspect that is the most important? There are actually many and you are about to learn the secrets that make a profile stand out.

Take the time to really consider each word that you put down on your profile. The only way for others to get to know you is through your profile, at least for now. Therefore, you must provide them with necessary and accurate information.

What's important to say? What shouldn't you say?

White Lies Never Hurt Anyone

As you create your profile, you may be tempted to fudge it just a little. After all, small little white lies never hurt anyone, right? Although you may be tempted to do this, whatever you do, don't do it. This is a huge mistake.

Lies that you tell here will be the foundation of why your online dating relationship does not work and fails miserably. The fact is that if you lie in this regard, big or small, you will find yourself facing trust issues down the road with those that just do not believe you.

Keep yourself honest throughout your profile. If you cannot answer a question honestly, then do not fill it in. If you are starting to fall for someone and they find out that you lied, it is over before it even had a chance to be successful.

Key Tips for Writing Your Profile

Writing your profile is one of the most important things that you will do in online dating. To be successful, you will need to write a profile that is geared towards several key aspects.

1. You should always be positive and even up beat in your profile. If you are positive, you will attract many more people to you than if you are negative. Do not use negative wording in any aspect of your profile. Do not write words like "hate" in your profile. Instead, mention something that is better. Instead of saying "I hate jazz" say "I like rock."

2. Make sure your sense of humor comes through. If you are someone that is interested in finding a person that is boring,

raise your hand. Most people are looking for someone interesting and funny. If you do have a sense of humor, make sure it comes through. Yet, only do this in a positive manner as you do not want to insult anyone either.

3. Take the time to read through posting requirements and rules before posting your profile. If you do not do this, you could find yourself facing losing your profile instead of being able to use it to launch your online dating career.

4. Don't be overly picky. If you write in your profile that you are only interested in successful men/women that work in high paying jobs you are less likely to get any results. Why? In this case it looks like you are hard to please and that perhaps you are out for someone that has money. Nevertheless, be open-minded about the qualifications that you put out there.

5. Don't be arrogant. Arrogant people are self-centered and not liked by the masses.

It is important that your profile is upbeat and positive.

First Impressions Matter

When it comes to finding someone online to date, get to know, even to marry, you need to be sure that your first impression is a good one.

It is crucial in online dating to give a good first impression more than anywhere else.

The other person does not see you in person.

You can't explain something to them unless they ask which most will not.

You can't charm them with a smile, not physically anyway.

What's more is that they can easily go off and find someone else to contact and get to know within 30 seconds of dropping by your profile.

Your first impression is a critical aspect of the online dating process and you can make it even more beneficial by simply insuring that you come through smiling, on the web of course!

Let's learn how you can do that.

Details About You

When writing your profile, one of the key things you will need to provide about yourself are the details. There are two types of people that mess this up here. There are those that provide way too much information, overwhelming anyone that is reading it and even driving them away.

Then, there are those that do not provide nearly enough information and those individuals are the ones that never get contacted because the reader was, well, bored with the profile and moved on.

You do not want to be these people. Instead, you want to be the person that provides just enough information to draw someone in and then give them something to wonder about. Provide them with a tease to lure them in.

In addition, your goal is to create a first impression that will allow them to smile when they finish reading the profile. They should walk away from the internet and remember your name or something in your online dating profile that sticks out.

Why do this? Because it will draw them back to you and encourage them to call on you.

What you shouldn't provide is not as clearly defined. You should not relate too much personal information to those that are seeking you out. You defiantly should never tell anyone where you live, where you work, or any personal and physically identifying things about you. These things can help to identify you and can lead predators to your door.

So how do you go about writing your profile? Grab a piece of paper and pencil and get rid of distractions. Write down anything and everything that comes to mind about you that is positive.

Write down the things that you like, the things that you enjoy doing, and some of your characteristics: sports, cooking, music, religion, friends, family, pets, caring, reliable, funny, etc. The list can go on and on. Write down positive things about you just in general, without any purpose.

Now, take a look at your list. Which ones do you feel that you can put up online for everyone to see without being negative, without being too arrogant and without sounding silly?

Selecting the right characteristics is important. Now, let's turn this task around and write down the characteristics you are looking for in a significant other. Which ones come up this time? You should see some common characteristics in what you are looking for and who you are.

There are some very common terms that you will want to put in your profile, assuming that they are things that you are. Try to include any of these if they do in fact fit you in some way.

- Honest
- Hard working
- Fun
- Sincere
- Normal
- Employed

- Caring
- Dependable
- Good Listener
- Commitment
- Understanding
- Interesting

A Tip to Remember:

When you include the terms that you yourself listed about the person you want to find in your own profile, you are likely to find yourself with more opportunities to meet Mr. Right or Ms. Right.

When you do this, you allow for the doors to open just a bit wider for you.

Chapter 6: Choosing Your Profile Picture

If there is one tip that you can take away from this book it is to create a profile that is worthy of being read. Your profile needs to draw in the person reading it and make them want to hit the button to email you.

Does that sound overwhelming? It does not have to be. Now that you have done quite a bit of the writing for your profile, your next step will be to add pictures to your profile.

Pictures? No way!

Before you run off and hide, adding pictures to your profile is a sure way to get more people to read and see that profile. If you want them to actually come to your profile and email you, you are going to have to lure them in. Pictures allow you to do this easily.

Not just any pictures work. There is a fine line of what will and what will not work and that's what you will need to understand to actually benefit from pictures.

What Pictures Say

Pictures are another essential element to the successful online dating profile. Pictures speak for themselves. They allow people to see who you really are. Believe it or not, people are not necessarily looking at your beauty and your waist size but rather they are looking at who you are in those pictures.

Important Tip:

Always make sure that the pictures you place in your profile are ones that show who you really are, not something that you are not.

To do this, you will first want to get together a whole group of pictures and decide what they can offer to your profile. Here are some picture qualities to look for.

- The picture should show you happy or at least in a good mood.
- The best pictures for a profile should show you doing things that you enjoy.
- Good pictures are those that show you with friends and family, having fun.
- Pictures of you do not have to be full body but they should be natural, not really posed pictures unless they are enhancing to you.
- Natural pictures allow others to see who you really are rather than what you look like posed.

There are plenty of things to think about when it comes to pictures for your profile but you should not get overwhelmed by it.

Do not focus on what you look like and if your hair is perfect. Remember, natural pictures are the most ideal choices.

You should choose pictures that show you doing things that you enjoy too. If you like to hike, why not include a couple of pictures of you and your friends hiking? If you like work in an office, you can show a picture of you taken at work, as long as you are happy at work.

The pictures that you place in your profile can be added in many ways. Always include those that are clear and are well done. Make sure that the picture at the front is the very best one of you.

Picture Warnings

Pictures are another first impression element. With that said, you already should be taking a second look at your profile's pictures. They should show you being true to yourself, not posing doing something you hate to do.

- The picture should not provide any negativity in them as these will not enhance your profile or draw others to you.
- Keep sad circumstances out of the pictures that you put up.
- Do include some pictures of you alone rather than just of you and friends. If you always include a friend, the person reading your profile may think you just do not have enough time for them in your busy, friend dominated life.
- Embarrassing pictures should not be included in your profile.
- Keep the sexy poses out of your profile too. You do not want to give the wrong impression. Believe it or not, this will push people away from you!

Chapter 7: What Are People Looking For?

At this point, you have a pretty great profile shaping up. That's the foundation of your online dating adventure hands down. Now, we need to take a minute to talk about what others are looking for in online dating partners across the board.

No matter who you are, you are looking for someone that is just like you.

In other words, people are looking for normal people. There is no one out there that is looking to hook up with someone that is too complex, too busy, too overwhelming, or someone that is too above them.

Sure, every guy says they want that hot model with all of the best figures, but the bottom line is that they are really looking for someone that is more normal that happens to be pretty.

How can this be? Doesn't everyone think about looks first in this world?

In reality, people are looking more for those that are normal and just like them because they do not want to feel or end up being rejected. We all fear rejection and at the level of online dating, it is the same.

Think about all the times that you have gone out and thought, "She's pretty, I would never have a chance with her." Or other such comments. For that reason, girls and guys out there should keep in mind that their profile and their pictures in the profile should be, beyond everything else normal.
Don't try to make yourself look like a supermodel because you end up looking fake.

Don't try to increase your importance by saying that you have a different job than you do.

Don't say you have special characteristics when you really do not.

People are looking for other normal people.

Your important tip here is that if you wish to have someone email you or contact you, you should come across as a normal person that is happy and positive. That's going to reel them in. But, not just in the way of your profile and your pictures, but throughout online dating.

Once you actually get into the dating scene, you will find that there are going to be opportunities to chat with others. In short, you will want to come across as being able to talk to anyone in the right manner.

Most commonly, people will respond to you through an email. Or, even better, you will respond to them in an email. You may find some will instant message you as well. Any of these methods is fine as long as you project a good first impression.

Relax, It's Okay!

When it comes to talking to others about who you are and what you are like, follow the same techniques in regards to being positive, normal and coming across as someone that is trustworthy and honest. Be yourself and just be normal.

Chapter 8: Take Action and Initiate Contact

When it comes to finding someone in the online dating world, the big secret is this: don't wait for them to come to you. Let's play the numbers game here.

If you register with an online dating website that has several thousand different users on it, what are your chances of standing out? What are the chances that you will actually have people emailing to talk to you?

There are two things to think about here.

1. What can you do to get others to find you in the most effective manner?
2. How can you find others and contact them to get things started?

Step 1: How They Will Find You

The first thing that you need to do is to determine how you can make other online dating users find you. Remember, this is a two-step process that cannot be minimized in just doing one or the other of these. If you truly want to succeed, these rules are necessary to follow.

One of the big aspects of this process you have already completed. That is that you have designed a profile that is perfect for those that are looking for you.

Your profile should:

- Depict you in your normal life and be honest to who you are.
- Provide an inside view as to who you actually are as well as what is important to you.
- Should be positive and allow you to come out looking interesting and someone fun to be with.

The next element is to insure that the words that you use within the profile are going to help to attract people to you. To do this, consider doing the following things.

First, make sure to add in the words that you would search for when looking for someone to date in the online dating world. Most of the online dating communities will have search features where individuals will type in certain things to find the person that they are interested in.

This can include such things as age, religion, and areas, but it is also going to include some pretty important other words. Remember, whatever words you would use to find someone else are those that you want to use in your profile.

When an individual is looking for you, they will type in these words into the search field. If they are in your profile, guess who will show up as a possible person that they will match with?

YOU!

This method will enhance how many people that are looking for the qualities that you possess to actually find you. If you just put in the average thing, you are less likely to be found in all of those millions of people. As frustrating as that sounds, it's just the way that the system works. Luckily, you have been shown how to improve your odds in the online dating world.

The more unique words and interesting things you add to your profile, the better. The more details you provide the better. Yet, do not go overboard in describing everything about you.

Step 2: Finding Those You Are Interested In

Don't run, you have to take this step too. Again, the odds are that you will need to do whatever it takes to contact and work with someone that is interested in finding you. You will have to make that first move and make it happen.

It does not have to be nerve racking or difficult do this. Email makes the whole process easier.

Important Tip:

Be the person that you are to your best friend when contacting someone else. Don't wait until they come to you. They are too worried to take this first step too.

Now, the first thing you need to do here is to find others that are potentially interesting people. What do you look for in an online profile? Well, we just went through an entire chapter about how to write a winning profile. Now, you need to reverse it.

Use the searches that are provided by the online dating sites. Look for unique characteristics. Instead of saying you are looking for someone that is smart, find someone that has a college degree or someone that likes to read. Keep in mind that too many specific things can keep you from meeting many people that could fit within your life very nicely.

You need to insure that you are scanning through profiles carefully. Again, positive people that have a great profile are the ones to go to. Why? They have taken the time and committed at least a few minutes to developing a profile that is interesting. In other words, they are interested in online dating and making an effort.

You should read through their profile and then decide if they are someone that you would be interested in.

When you find someone that sounds interesting, stop for a minute and ask yourself if you could see yourself with this person, really. There is no sense in wasting your time on someone that you won't like for a major reason. Yet, if you are not sure, they are worth contacting.

Yes, contacting. The next chapter will help you with writing that first email.

CHAPTER 9: SENDING EFFECTIVE EMAILS

You have found a few people online that seem to be nice enough to talk with and maybe you are considering emailing them.

Who are you kidding! If you want to be successful with online dating, you have to make the first move, no matter who you are, girl or boy!

After you have found a few people to contact, you will want to write out that first email. Of course, you could instant message them, but that puts you and them more on the spot and may not be as wise of a choice at this point.

Instead, craft an email.

Email tips include:

- In your email, make sure you provide your name and where you found their profile.

- Keep the tone of the email upbeat and interesting, not dull and boring.
- A quick note is fine as long as it begins a conversation and is not just, "I saw your profile, email me." This will not work.

One thing to keep in mind in the content of the email you send is just what you will say. You should introduce yourself and provide some information about you. Tell them your name, your age and things about who you are. You can tell them such things as your interests and your characteristics.

Do not bore them, but provide them with some information so that they can begin to build a bit more of an idea of who you are. You want them to be able to remember you from one email to the next one that you send. Give them something to think about!

Next, make sure that you provide some comments about their profile. You can say that you saw they liked to hang out at the beach. Perhaps this is something that you share in common and therefore you can share that.

Find some common connection between their profile and your interests. When you do that, you form a bond with them that can grow into something much more positive. It helps to develop a conversation which is something you have to have to get a response from them.

Finally, make sure to include in your email a few questions to get the conversation going. Keep this to about two to three but make sure they are on different subjects. You can ask them about their day to day life, about their pets, about the places that they grew up, etc. Whatever you can find that is common ground to link you with them.

By doing this it will allow you to do one thing perfectly. That is, it will allow you to develop a relationship with them even at a very basic level. They will now have something to say back to you and things can begin to take shape.

That first email is worrisome, but once it is sent, things will begin to roll from there.

Chapter 10: A Little Bit of Charm Can Go a Long Way

In addition to sending out that first email, there are going to be times when you will need to actually talk to the other person. It may be just through the email at first, but will likely lead to instant message conversations and then to the phone.

One thing that you will want to make sure comes through in the entire process is your charm. No matter if you are a guy or the girl; you want to give off the right impression to them through the words that you use. Often time's people do not realize that words typed do not have the same feeling as words said. Therefore, you need to insure you use the right wording for true success.

For example, you want to make sure you are saying things that will keep the conversation going in a positive direction. You will need to choose your words wisely and accurately. Do not say things sarcastically unless you are sure that they will get it. It could easily turn out to be an insult or misunderstanding.

One of the largest mistakes with online dating is letting the conversation go. People will find themselves talking to someone through an email only to turn around and stop.

You need to insure that you say things that will bring up new things and keep things moving. Many relationships fail because someone has stopped communicating.

It Doesn't Stop There

Emails and instant messages are only good for a short period of time. The fact is that you will need to take it to the next level at some point. Again, girls and guys can do and should do this. Don't wait for someone else to make the right move.

If you wait, you may lose out altogether on the relationship after relationship.

If you feel that it is time to give her or him a call, than do it. In fact, if you let this extend past the first few emails, then you may have lost your shot. So, when you have spent some time talking back and forth and still are interested in this person, send them an email asking for their phone number.

It is okay to ask for their phone number after the first email but your odds increase if you wait until the second or third email.

The goal is to get their number and make the call. Calls lead to the next level which is meeting in person. That is what you set out to do, right?

Saying the Right Things

Are you worried about saying the right thing? Perhaps you are thinking that there is not going to be a way for you to make that call or to contact that person. You just would not know what to say.

If you take on this mentality, you are going to find yourself never getting anywhere when it comes to online dating. Instead, use the following tips to help you get through the rough spots.

1. Don't psych yourself out by thinking about someone as your potential boyfriend/girlfriend or husband/wife/ Approach your contact or early conversations as just meeting someone new that may turn out to be a friend or maybe something more.

2. Next, really think about what you are writing. Ask about things that are things that you are really interested in. If they made note of taking several trips in the last few years, ask them where they went and what they enjoyed on those trips. Find things that you really want to know about.

3. To be positive and have your personality come through, add your own comments and thoughts in. If they went hiking in an area that you did, simply comment about how when you went there, your favorite part was at xyz point.

4. Compliments work magic on people. You want to make sure that people feel good about themselves when talking to you. You should say something like, "I thought your profile was really interesting. You have a talent for writing!" Compliments always bring a smile as long as they are in good taste and kept to just a few.

5. Remember, if this does not work out with them, there are plenty of others out there. There is nothing on the line here. The only thing that is at risk is your ability to go out and find someone for you.

Chapter 11: Don't Let Fear Paralyze You

There are plenty of times when you will find yourself dealing with something you do not want to do. But, before you write off online dating as being something that is just too hard to do, realize that the process is full of rewards.

How will you do at this online dating adventure? Only you can really tell and come up with a solution for that. The fact is that there are plenty of opportunities to find success, but you have to provide the commitment to it to actually allow it to happen.

Giving It Your All

One thing that you will need to realize is that it may take countless opportunities to find that right person for you. In other words, from the start you should realize that you may have to fail a few times before you will find that one person that is right for you.

Yet, to make this a better situation for you, think of it in a different manner.

Instead of thinking of someone as a potential girlfriend/wife or boyfriend/husband, think about them as merely just a person that is a friend.

When you do this, you take off a lot of pressure which you just do not need to deal with. You are simply out there, on the web, looking for people that will qualify to be your friends first.

Dealing with Rejection

It is bound to happen. You are going to find situations in which you are going to be rejected. You are going to find opportunities when you will succeed too. Yet, dealing with rejection may cause you to want to throw in the towel. Before, you do that though; think about all of the benefits that have been discussed. You can make this work.

If you find yourself facing rejection from those that you contact, realize that it is more than likely something that is going to happen because you and that person do not share enough in common.

If you do not do the things that we have been covered in this book, you are sure to find yourself dealing with rejection more often than not. So, make sure you have followed the advice from this book. Is your profile current and accurate? Is it appealing? Does your profile contain information that would interest others? Are you holding up the conversation on your end? Are you taking things to the next step?

Not sure why you keep getting rejected? Ask a good friend that you trust to read through your profile. They can objectively tell you just how accurate it really is. Have them answer these questions.

- Does it portray you in the right light?
- Is it portraying you in a positive light that is interesting?
- Are they drawn in to it?
- What's missing?

Take their input constructively and make the necessary changes. What do you have to lose?

Chapter 12: Meeting for a First Date

Part of online dating is meeting other people. You will need to invest the time necessary in finding others and getting to know them. If things are progressing well you will eventually want to meet them. But for some, this can be one of the most nerve wracking aspects of online dating.

All of the same things that applies to standard dating relates to online dating when it comes to meeting others. Nevertheless, it is a very different situation indeed.

There are many important things that you need to take into consideration.

Safety

When it comes to meeting for a first date, safety has to be one of the largest concerns on your mind.

Here are a few very important rules that you need to keep in mind when it comes to meeting someone new for the first time.

- Meet in a public area. You should meet in an area that has other people in it. This way, you can easily stay safe with the public's watchful eye. Avoid temptations to leave these types of areas on the first date.

- Meet them someplace rather than allowing them to pick you up. This way, you have your own method of transportation for safety reasons.

- Make sure that you feel comfortable with them. If you do not like that they are touching you, tell them so. If this is a problem, leave.

- Tell someone where you are going and what your plans are.

- Stay in well-lit areas that feel comfortable to you. You should know the area at least somewhat.

Keeping yourself safe is very important and is a very necessary step in the process of online dating.

What if safety isn't an issue but you are with someone that you do not click with and really do not like? For these situations you need to have a backup escape plan.

You need to enlist a friend or a family member to help you. Tell them where you are going and what you will be up to. When a date is not go well, you need a way out and they are the person to help you.

Set a time for them to call you. This should be no more than an hour into the date. When they call you, you have the opportunity to end the date. Tell your date that something has happened and you need to leave. Be polite and apologetic if you like, but you are not obligated to answer questions or provide details. If you need to escape from the date chances are you have no interested in being friends with this person or ever seeing them again.

If all is going well, you can easily cut the conversation short and let them go. It's a great way to get out of a bad situation.

Meeting someone in person from an online dating site will usually determine if you both are interested in taking the relationship to the next level.

Just remember that meeting someone in person is another "first impression" opportunity. Take the time necessary to prep and make it a good one.

Chapter 13: Online Dating Tips to Remember

When it comes to online dating, the basics have been covered along with some great tips to help you achieve real success.

Let's sum up some of the best tips for you to remember when it comes to meeting people online.

First off, your profile; you know just how important it is and why you need it to be accurate. It is a tool that allows you to meet others that are like you and provide information about yourself.

- Positive, happy and inviting words should be used always!
- Use pictures that showcase you as happy and acting normally. Include several different, appealing shots.
- Place key words into the description of your profile so that those that are looking for your characteristics can find you. Remember, ask yourself what you are looking for.

Next, you need to take action and make the first move. Don't wait for others to find you. Seek them out and initiate contact. While your profile is designed to lure them in, you still need to get out there and find that perfect person. You can do!

Once you decide to contact someone, make sure that you ask questions, provide information about you and keep the conversation going. If you do not do this, you will find yourself wasting your time. Remember, within a few conversations through email or instant message, you need to ask for their number to keep things moving. If you or they get bored, the opportunity has been lost.

In addition, you need to realize that online dating is something that does take time to make happen. Therefore, you will need to dedicate yourself to crafting a profile that is worthy and keep at it even when you face rejection.

Chapter 14: Are Online Dating Tests Helpful?

One thing that we have not mentioned that can be of use to you is the online dating test. These tests are supposed to be compatibility tests that will help the online dating site pair you up with others that are just like you. Therefore, they are tools that can aid in providing you with help in finding the right person out there.

If you have selected to work with a good quality online dating website, these tests can be somewhat helpful. Yet, they are also misleading and can be completely thrown off by you.

If you decide to take and use them, which you should do, you will want to take a couple of things into consideration. First, make sure that you read through the process and really understand it. Short cuts leave you frustrated and wasting your time.

Second, make sure that you are taking the test honestly. There is no doubt that you can persuade the test in one direction or in the other. It happens quite regularly. We subconsciously allow ourselves to select a person that is what we think is right by simply answering questions in that manner. This allows for the test to become nothing but worthless.

Instead of doing that, what you really need to do is to answer each question honestly and after giving it a bit of thought. Otherwise, you will find yourself wasting time.

In addition, do not limit yourself by what the test results show. If you find someone that looks interesting to you, reach out and contact them. Dating tests can be helpful but just remember that they are not always accurate.

If you use it as a tool, it can help you greatly. Just do not rely solely on that test!

Chapter 15: Final Thoughts on Online Dating

One thing that about online dating is can be a whole lot of fun. Sure, there's effort needed on your part and you may not be ready to make a full commitment just yet. But think about the possibilities and opportunities that could come from it.

Creating a great profile for success is something that you can do one time and benefit from in the long haul. You do not have to do this each and every time that you log on or join a new site. Since you have designed it so well, people will find you easily and you will receive emails from others that are interested.

Remember that it is not all about what you look like or what job you have. People are looking for other people that are just like them: normal. Therefore, be honest in your profile and allow them to see just who you actually are. In addition, you will want to find a way to hold their interest and draw them in to you. If you want them to email you, be real and be approachable.

There is no denying that rejection is part of the online dating process. It's just the way it is. Yet, there is safety in knowing that rejection will come in the form of an email that can be easily deleted. Don't be discouraged because there is a database that is full of many more wonderful people that are looking to be, well to be with you. You are all there for the same reason: finding someone to love.

Use the tips and advice from this book to lead you down the road to successful dating on the web. Read it again and use it as a step-by-step method of getting your online dating adventure started.

MEET THE AUTHOR

Jane Wymer is known among her friends as "The Matchmaker." It's not just that she has a sense of who will "fit" together, although she definitely does. It's that she's a student of people, and over the years she's gained a lot of wisdom in what makes people datable. She has a kind spirit and is often able to gently help people recognize areas that need some work.

The child of two therapists, Jane has been helping people solve conflict since she could talk. She gave pep talks to stuffed animals and advice to her elementary school teachers. During high school, she observed that while her classmates were obsessing about looks, the thing that really drew people to one another was confidence. She was the person who helped all her friends find and keep relationships, but didn't have one of her own. For the longest time she was great at unraveling anyone's love life, but in her own she was the classic over-thinker. When she finally met her husband, Mr. Surely-He-Isn't-Right, his mantra to her was, "Less thinking, more trusting." And it worked!

She and Mr. Right-After-All just celebrated ten years of marriage. They have two beautiful pups and happily meddle in the lives of all their single friends.

More Books by Jane Wymer

How to Get Your Ex Back: Win Back Your Ex and Rebuild Your Relationship

www.ingramcontent.com/pod-product-compliance
Lightning Source LLC
LaVergne TN
LVHW021739060526
838200LV00052B/3358